Coloring Book for Adults and Kids
Beautiful and Cute Animals Pattern

Nisita Noojui

Coloring Book for Adults and Kids: Beautiful and Cute Animals Pattern

Copyright: Published in the United States by Nisita Noojui
Published October 2016

ISBN-13: 978-1539739821

ISBN-10: 1539739821

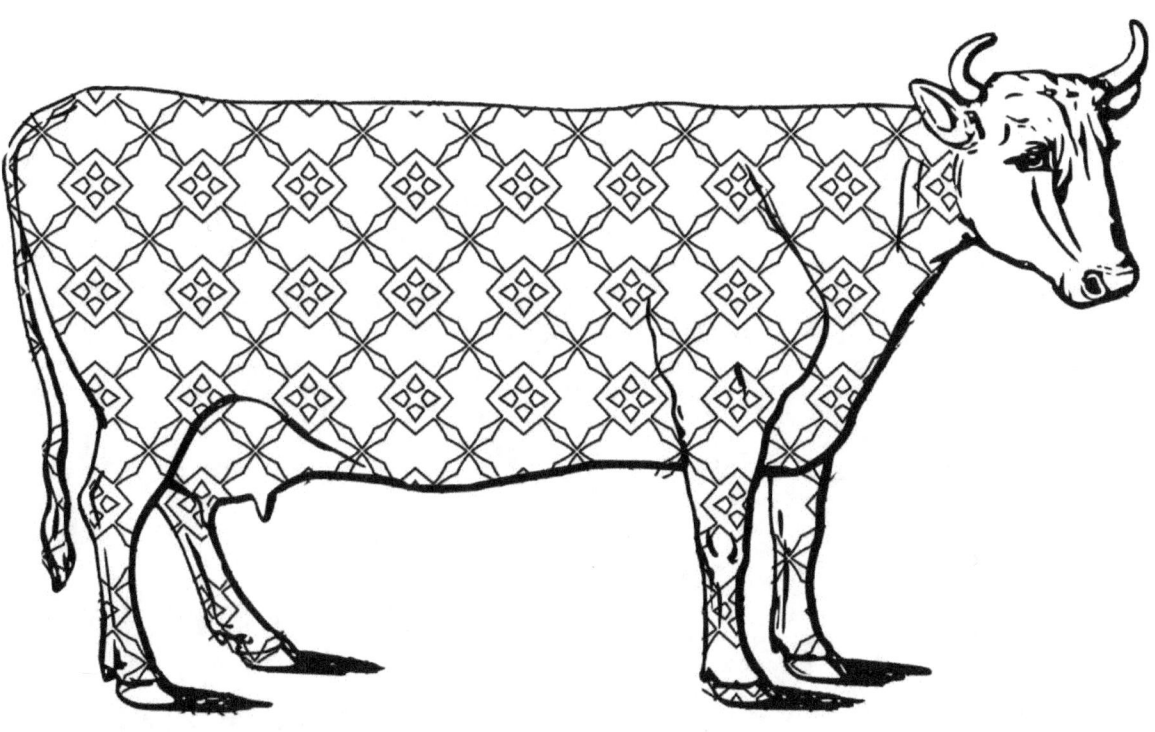

Thank you